THE 7TH DUCKLING

MEET THE 7TH DUCKLING

WRITTEN BY

LOIS SHUART

COPYRIGHT © 2025 BY LOIS SHUART

DEDICATION

I dedicate this book to Phillip J. Shuart, my husband,
who is the love of my life, and who is always filled
with positive support for me.

ACKNOWLEDGEMENT

Anne Helmstadter, Founder and CEO of The Story tImmersion Project, where hundreds of us are learning the craft of writing. Anne is my teacher and coach, who made a writing career within my grasp. Thank you to my schoolteachers who were always supportive of my writing and creativity. Many thanks to Liz Pearson, Alex D'Souza, and Tim Anderson of Kindle Direct Publishing Company, who are guiding me to make the dream of a children's series a possibility. There is always a village to make a writer.

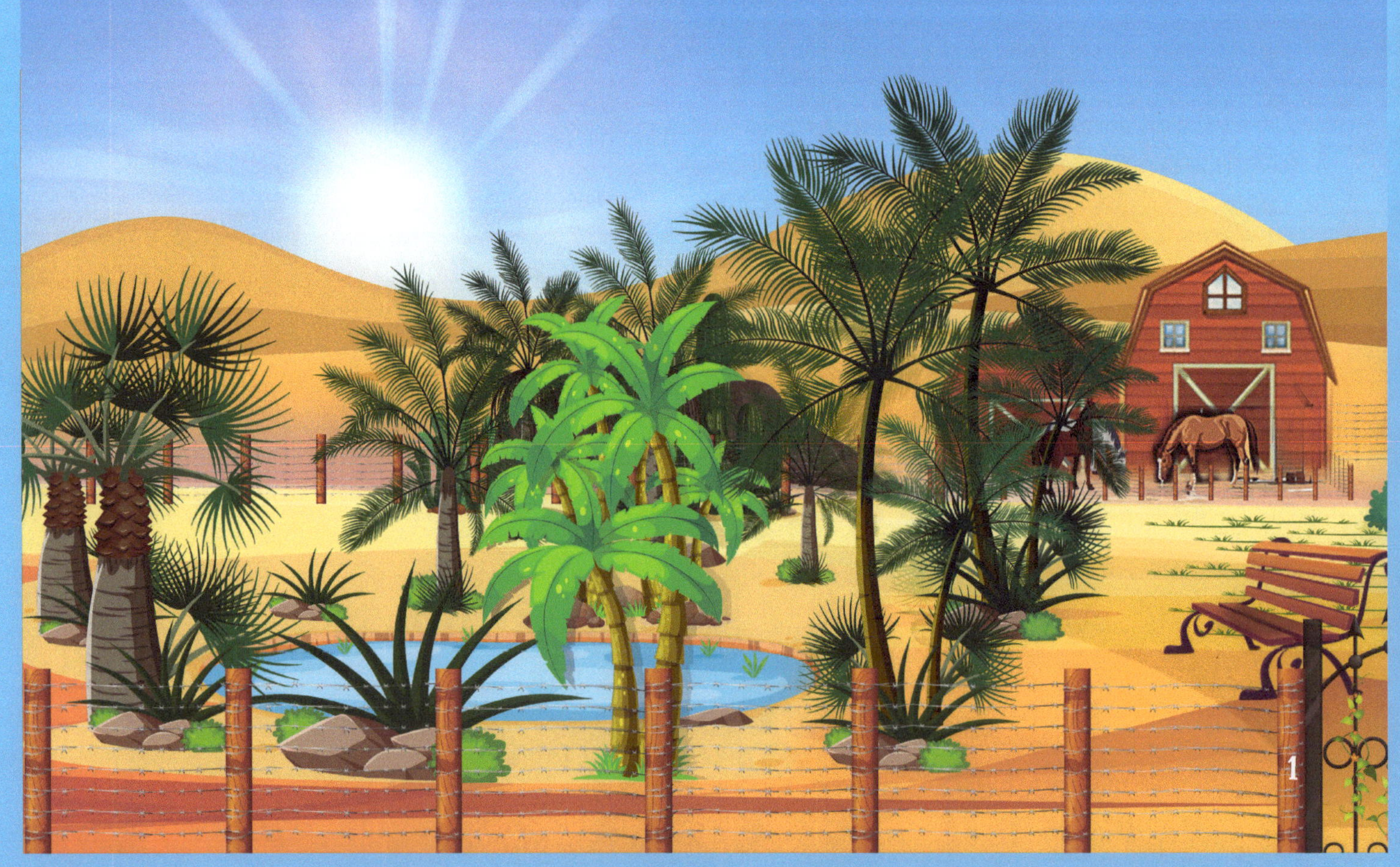

One Saturday morning, when the old lady of the ranch went out to feed her Hummingbirds, eight ducks waddled in through the front gate. There was a Mama duck, six tiny baby ducklings, and a seventh duckling that looked a little larger than the rest.

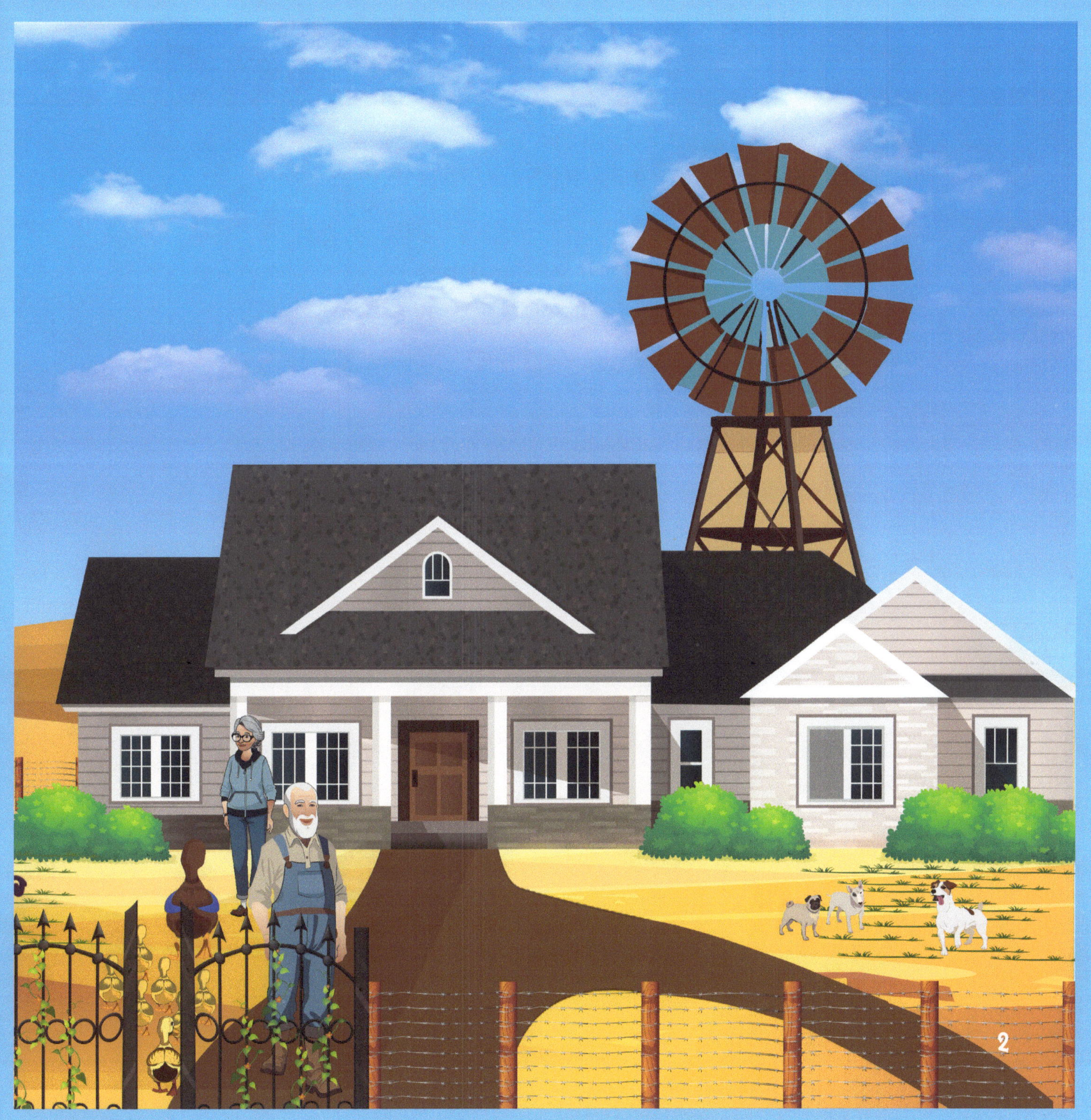

Mama duck marched them in single file, onto the sandy desert floor, and over to the pond, where she led them down the path, past the dock to the water. She was happy that they all obeyed and were now swimming in the cool water of the pond on such a hot day.

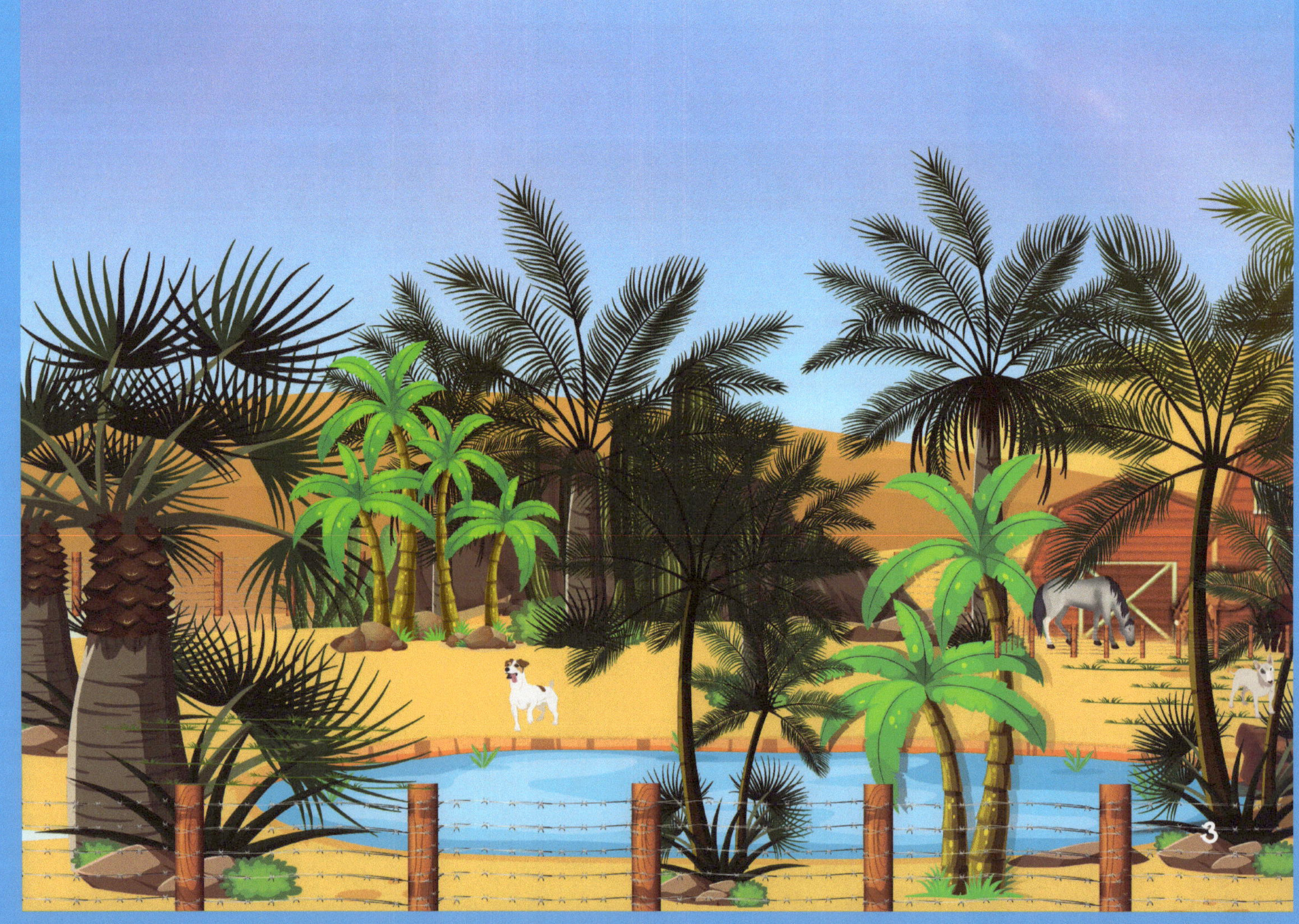

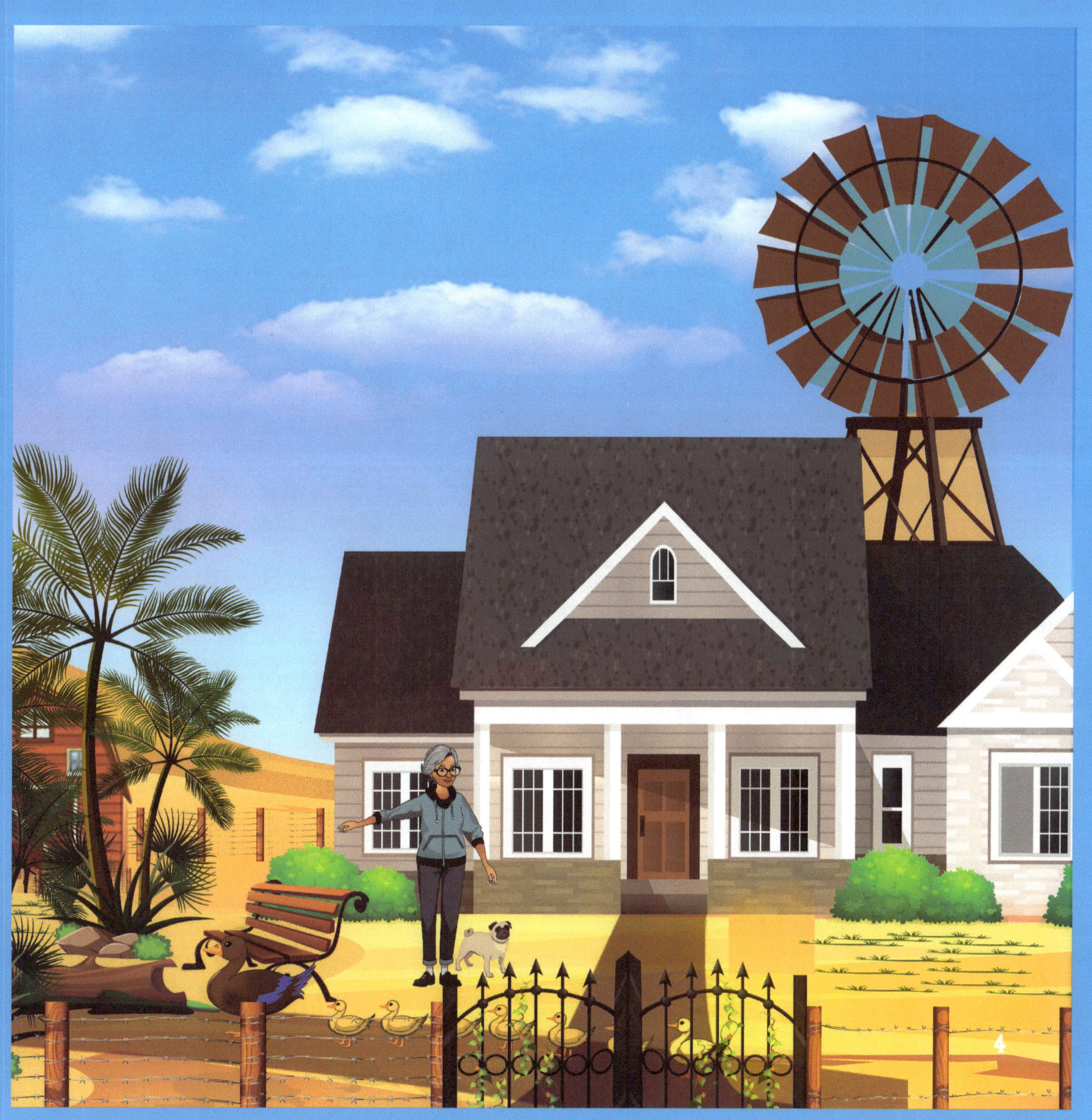

They could all swim quite well, but I think this day was about cooling off, getting a drink, and catching bugs. All the little ducks were trying hard to do just that. Mama swam all around them to keep them together.

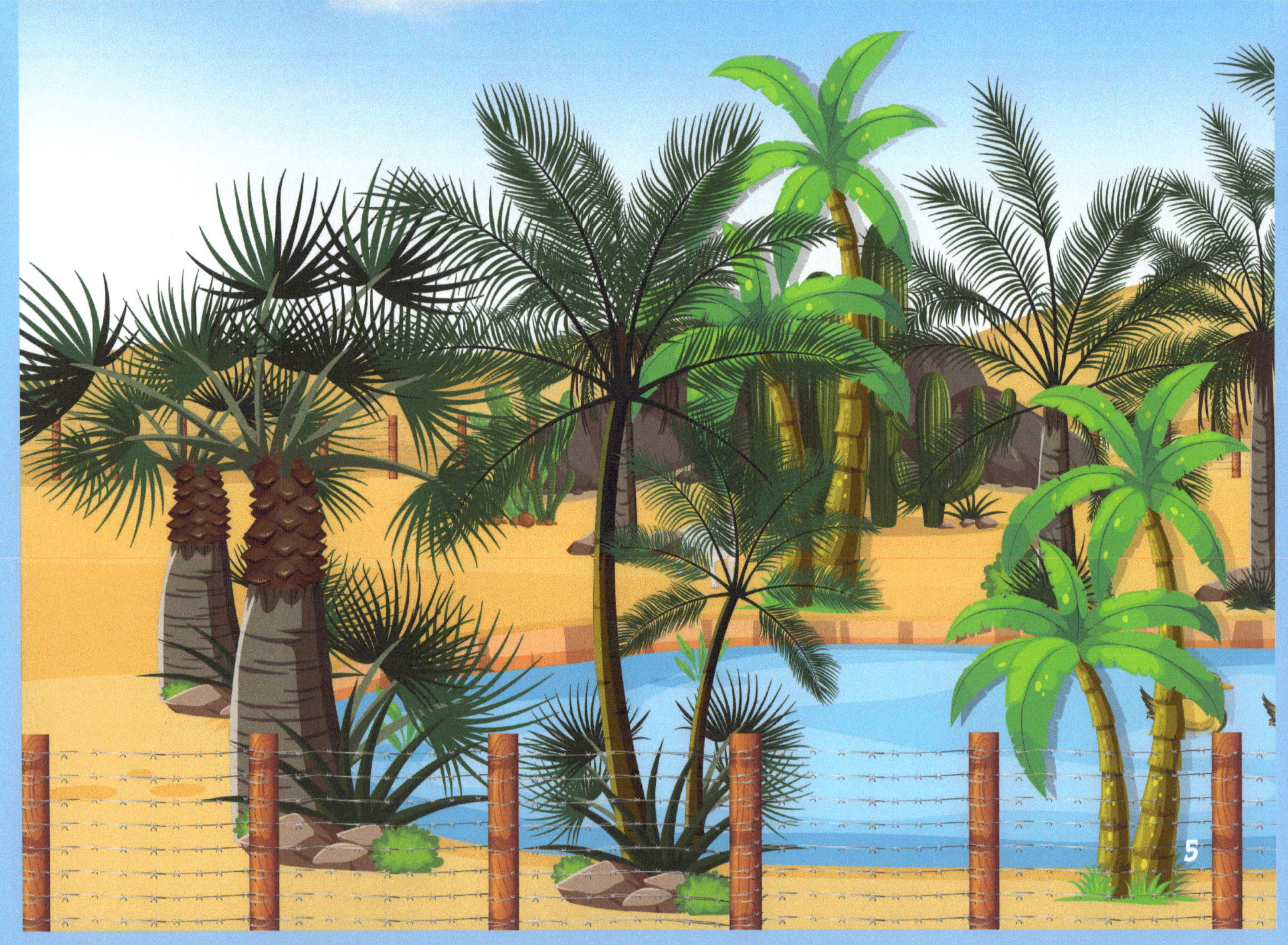

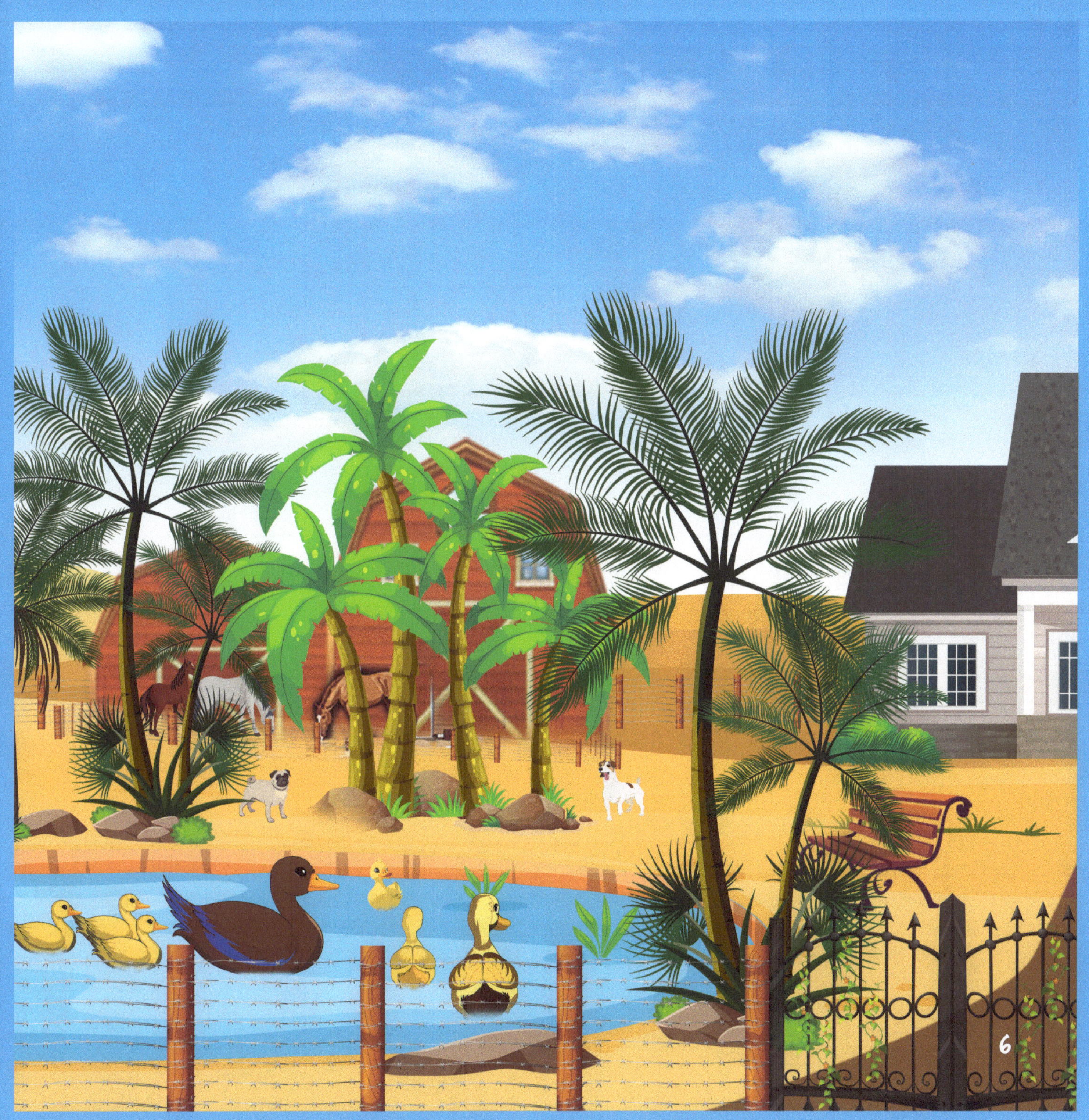

Mama showed them how to catch a bug that landed on the water and how to catch a bug flying nearby. The little old lady was quite pleased that she now had a family of ducks enjoying her pond. She quickly closed the gate so that no coyotes would come in to bother them.

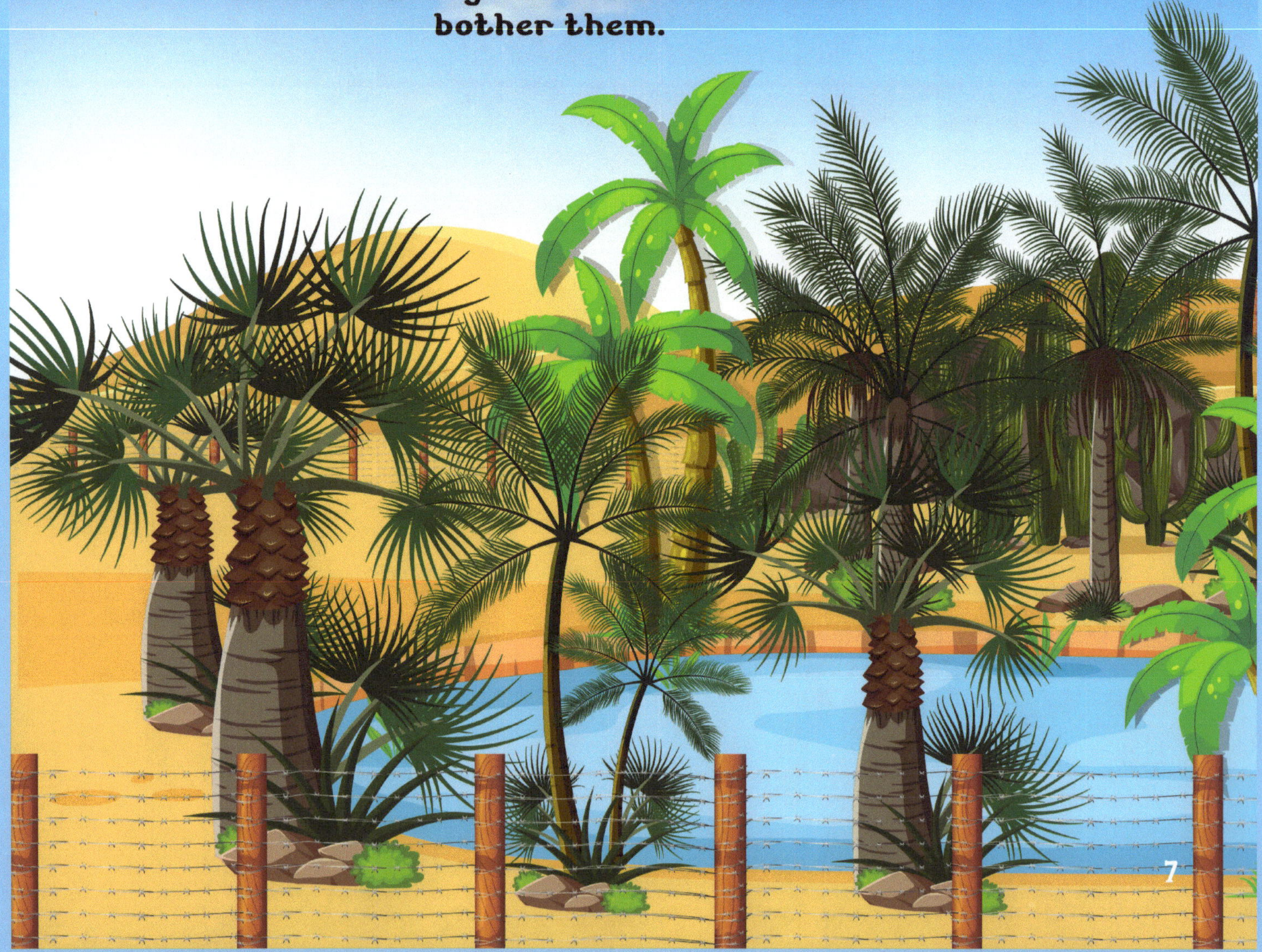

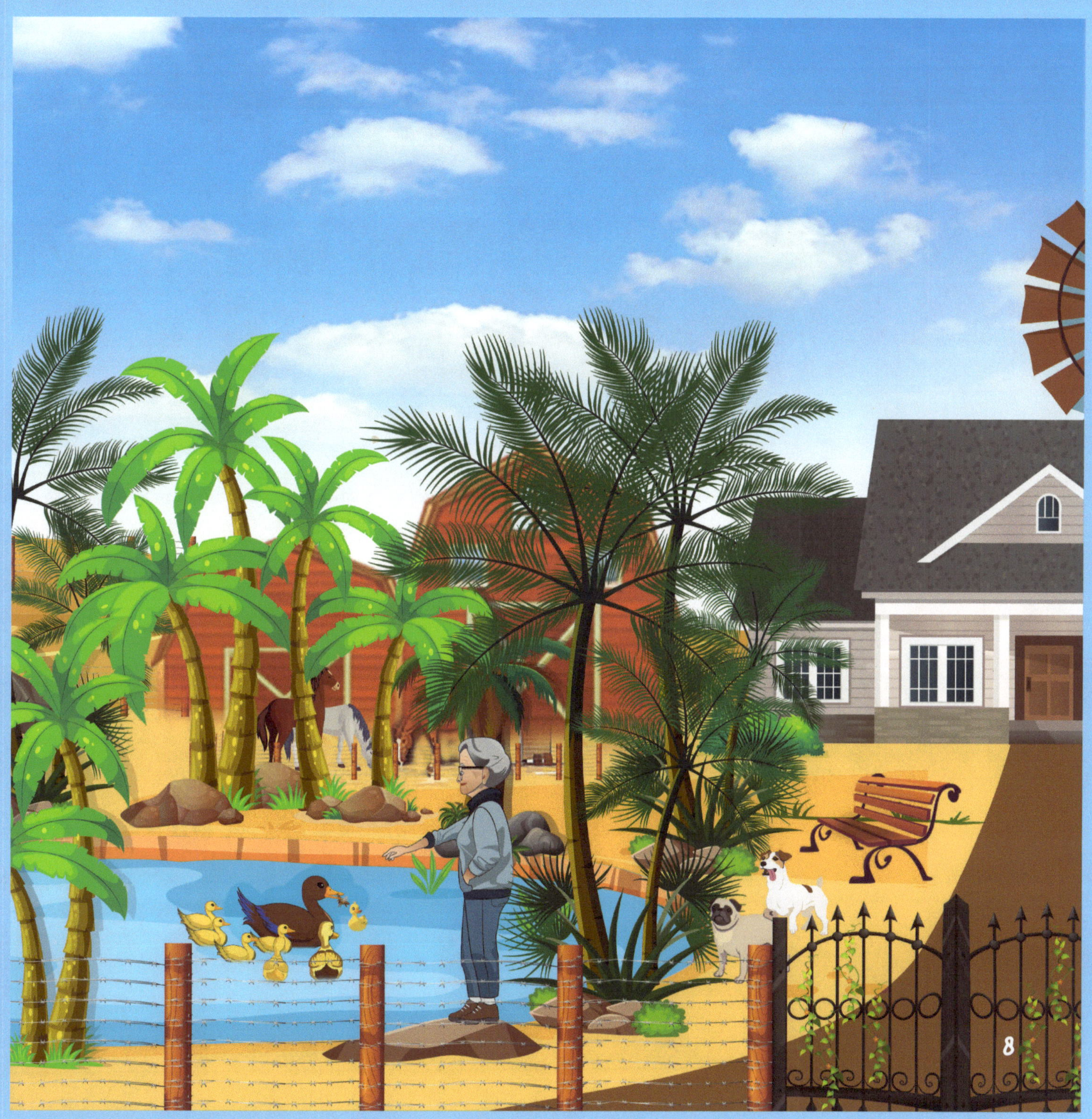

That same night, the little old lady went out to show her husband the new family at the pond. He, too, was happy about the ducks. He also mentioned that the last duckling looked much larger than her brothers and sisters. They said good night to the ducks and went off to feed the horses, and brought the dogs inside.

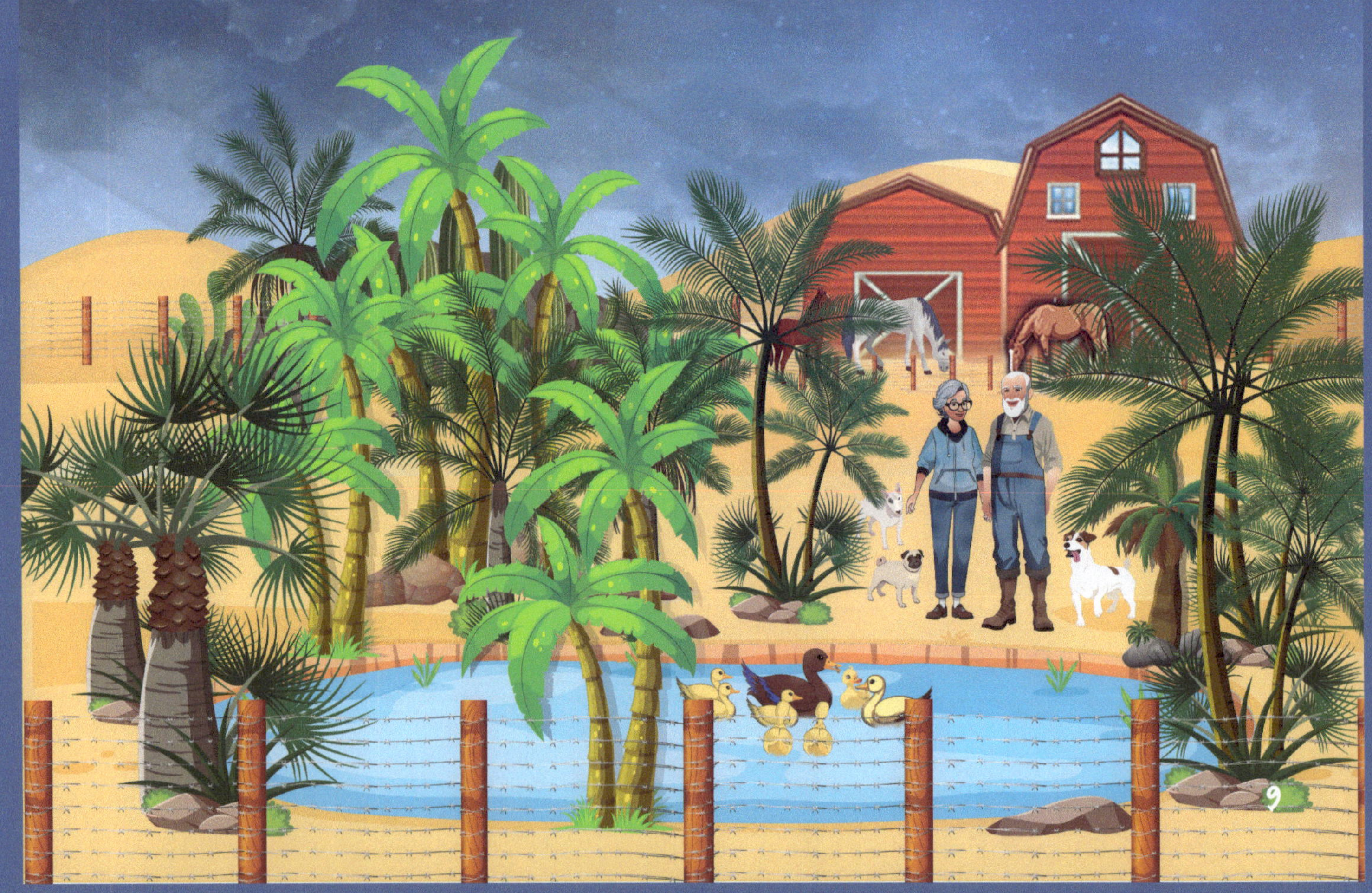

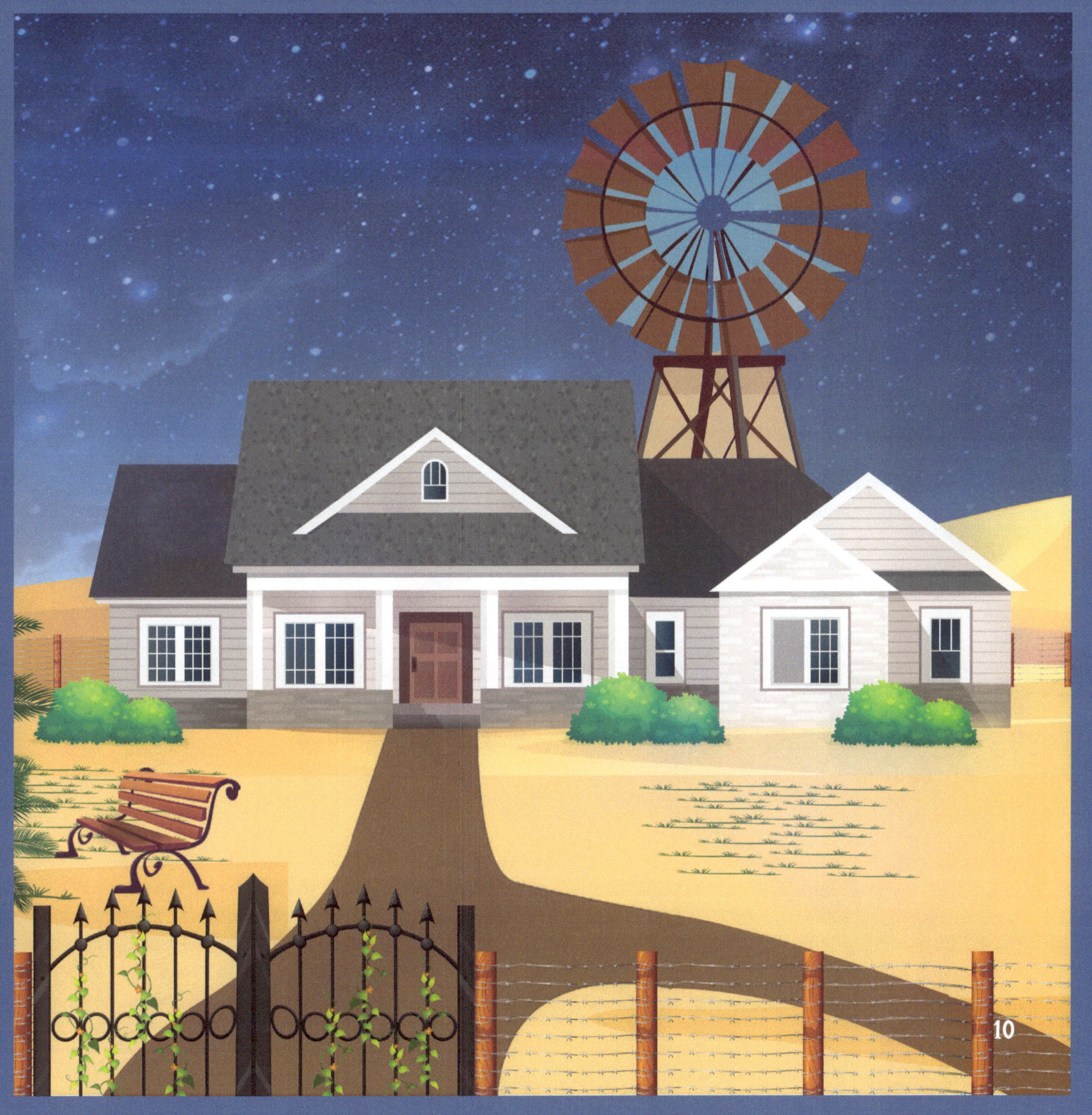

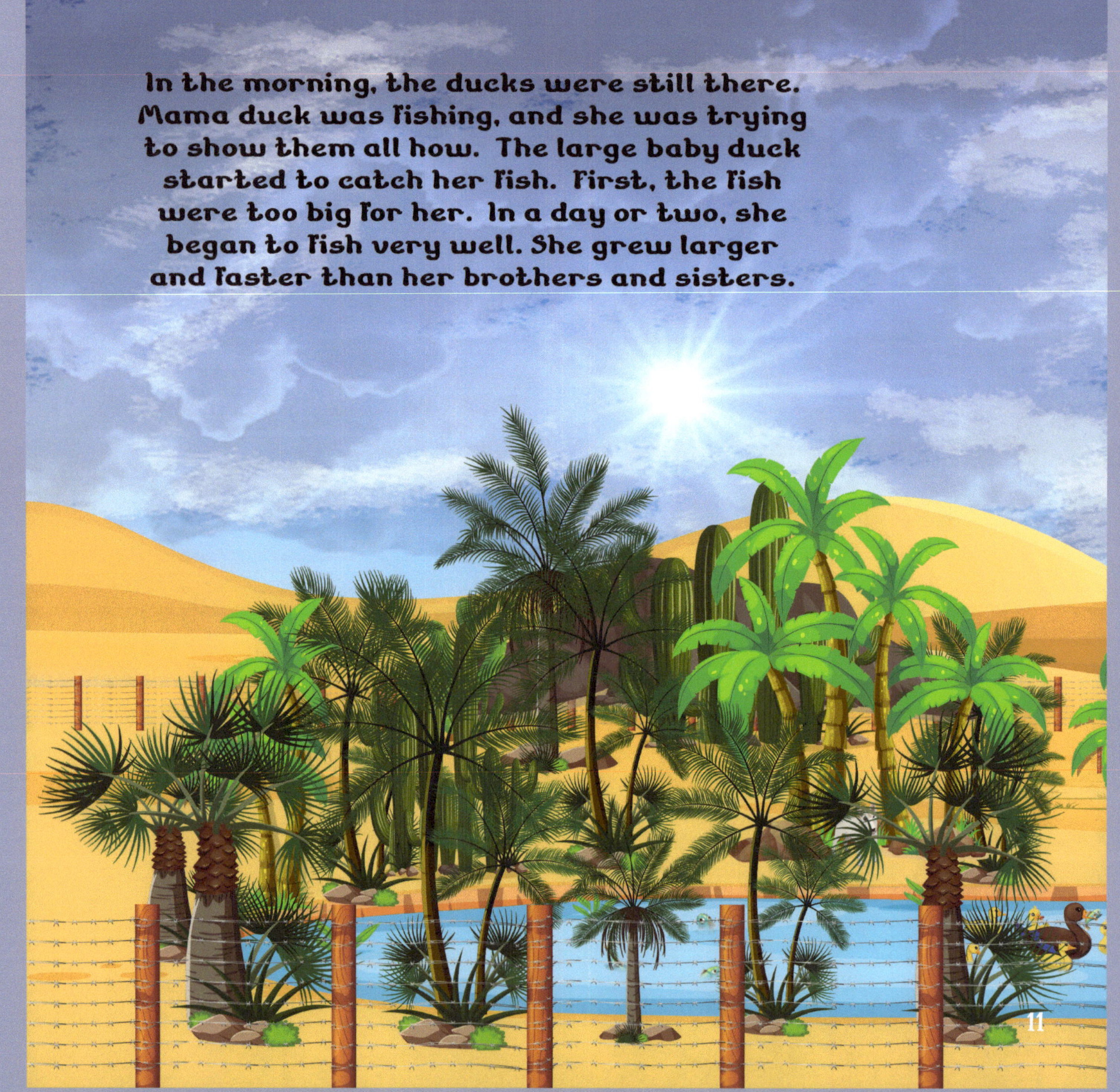

In the morning, the ducks were still there.
Mama duck was fishing, and she was trying
to show them all how. The large baby duck
started to catch her fish. First, the fish
were too big for her. In a day or two, she
began to fish very well. She grew larger
and faster than her brothers and sisters.

11

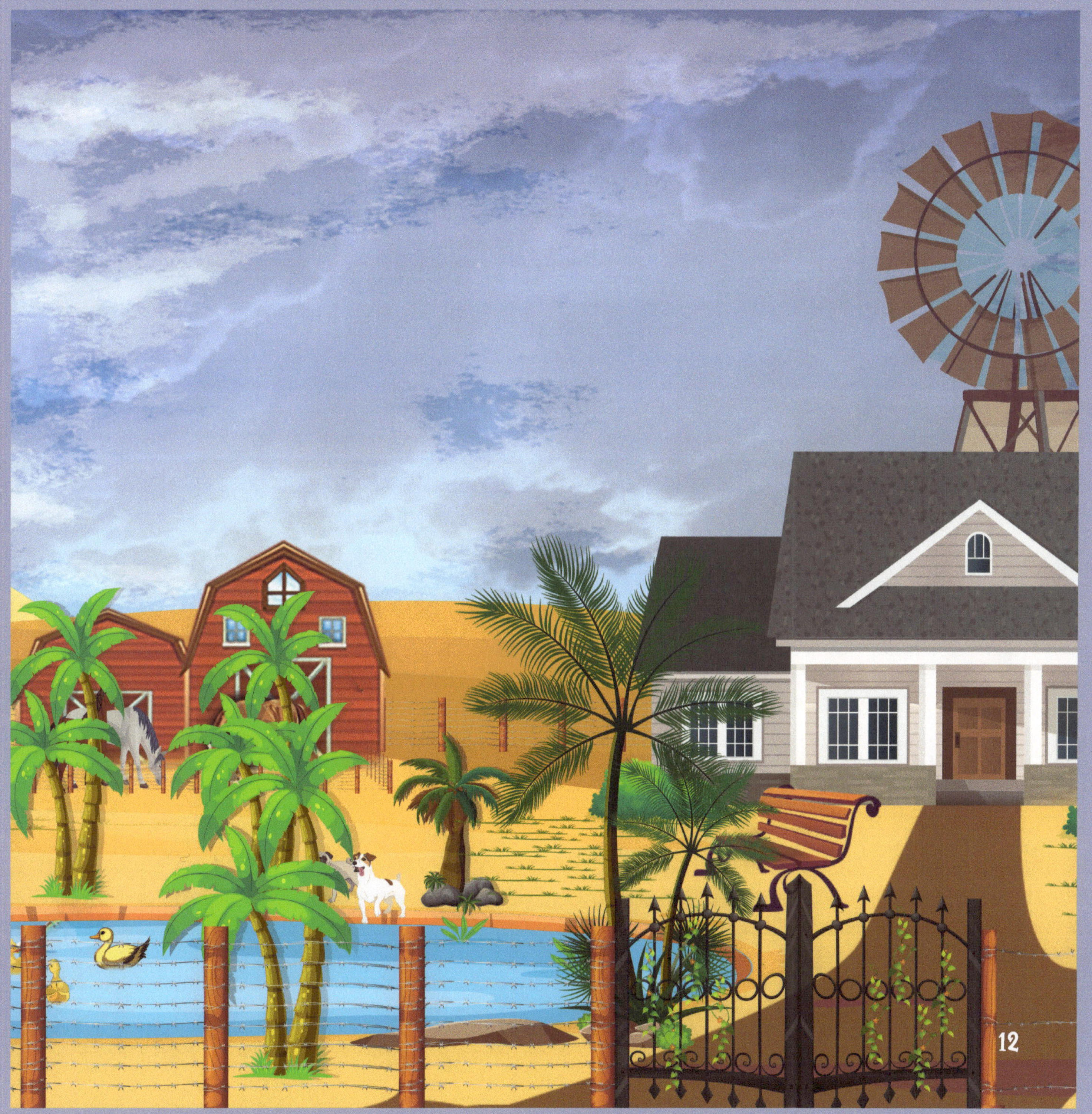

It was about week number two when
Mama duck did a strange thing. She left
the pond with the babies, in a row behind
her, and took a small walk about. The 7th
duckling did not follow. She happily stayed
in her pond and caught fish and bugs.
With the closed gate, she was safe.

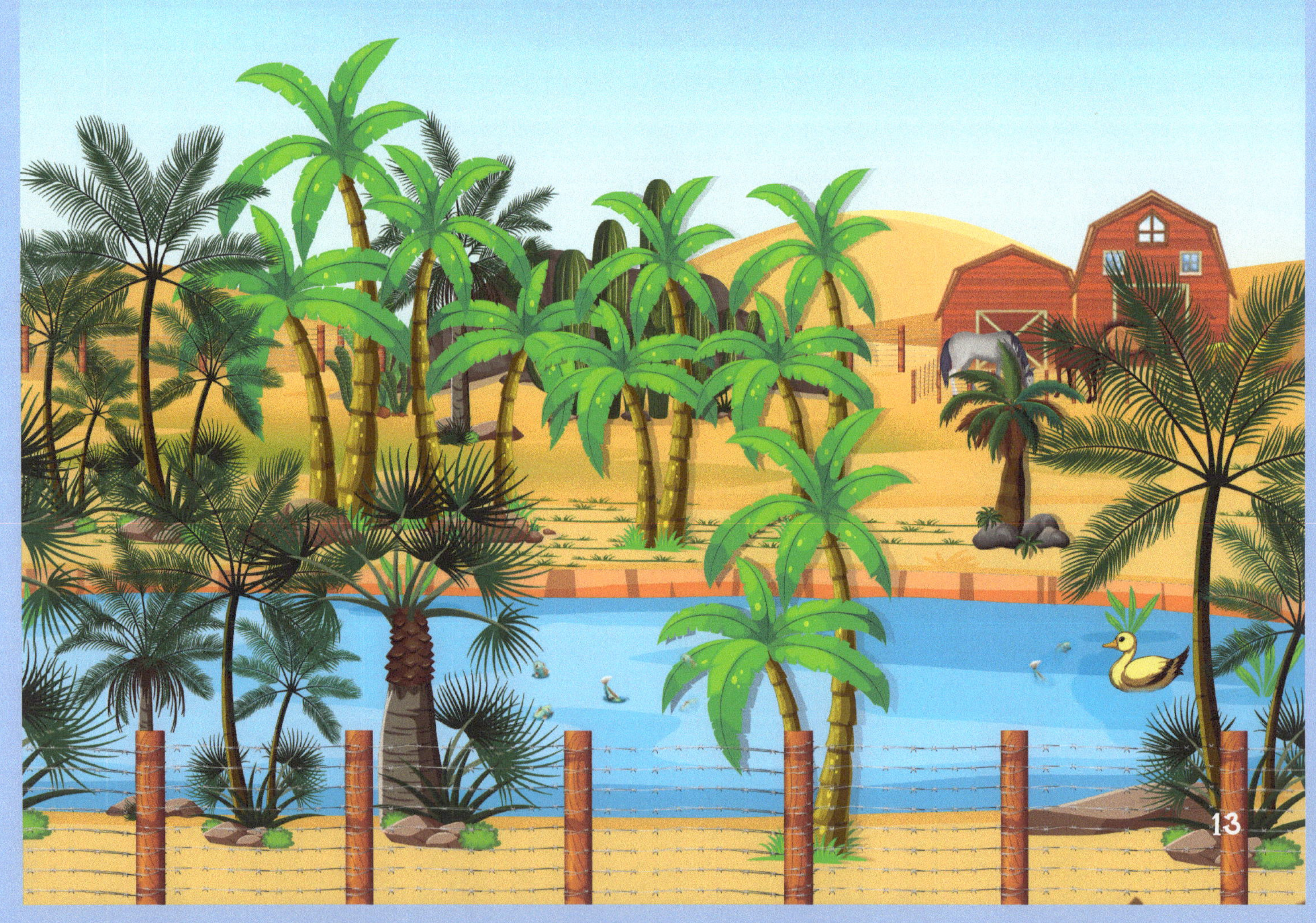

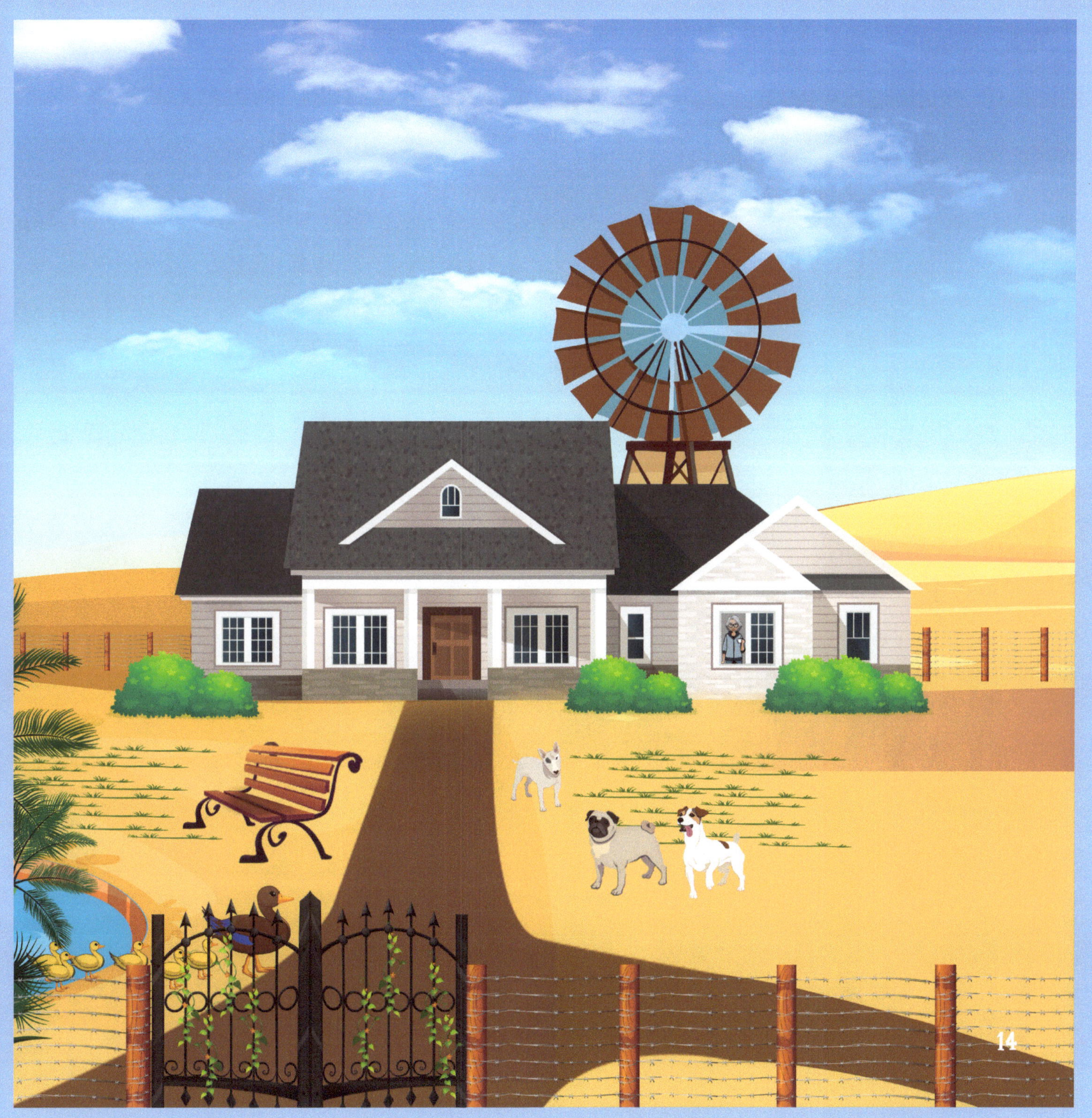

Early in the morning, the sun rose
above the pond, and there was the
7th duckling all alone. There weren't
any brothers and sisters, and the
Mama duck was nowhere to be seen.
The old woman was very upset.

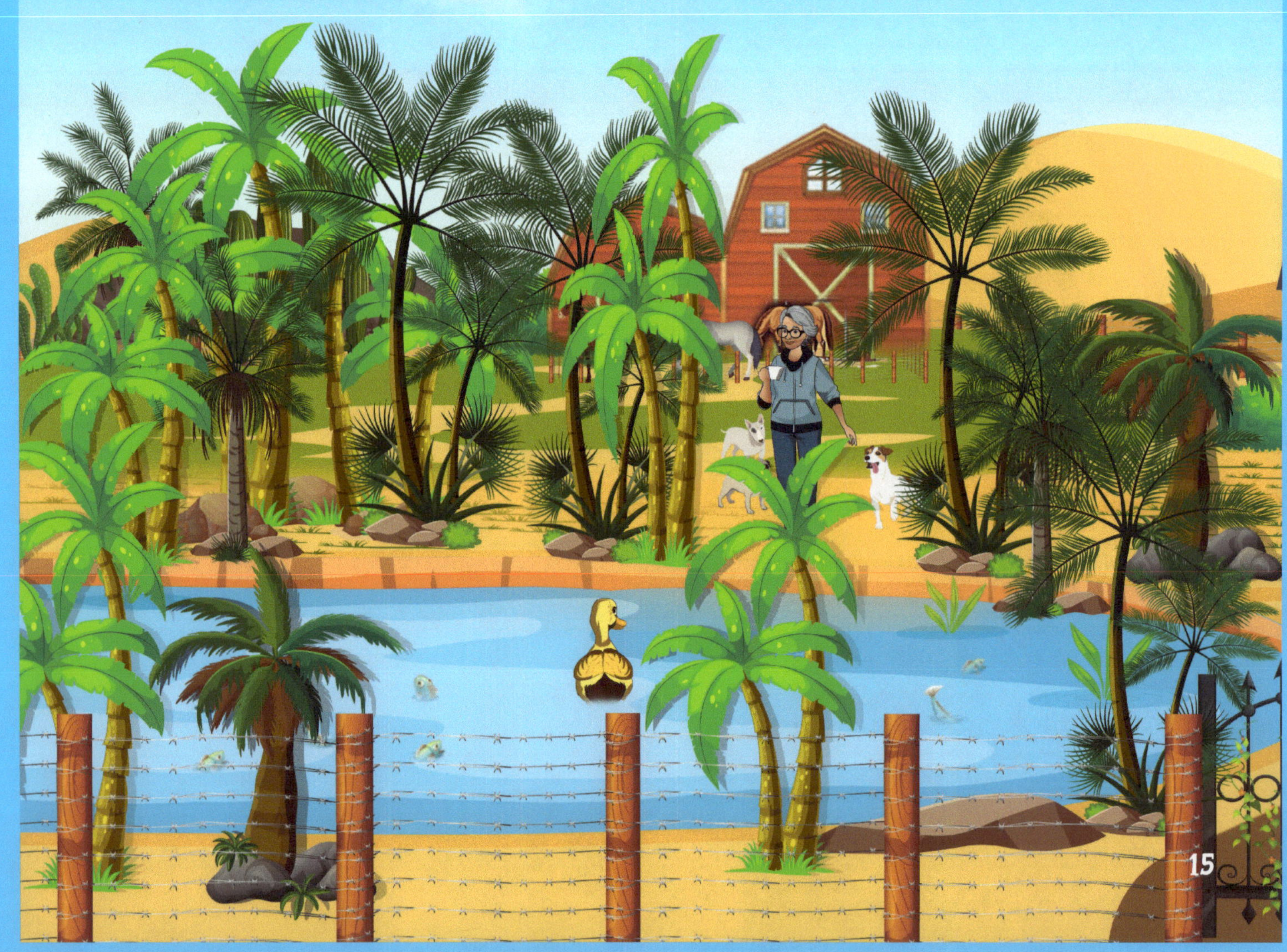

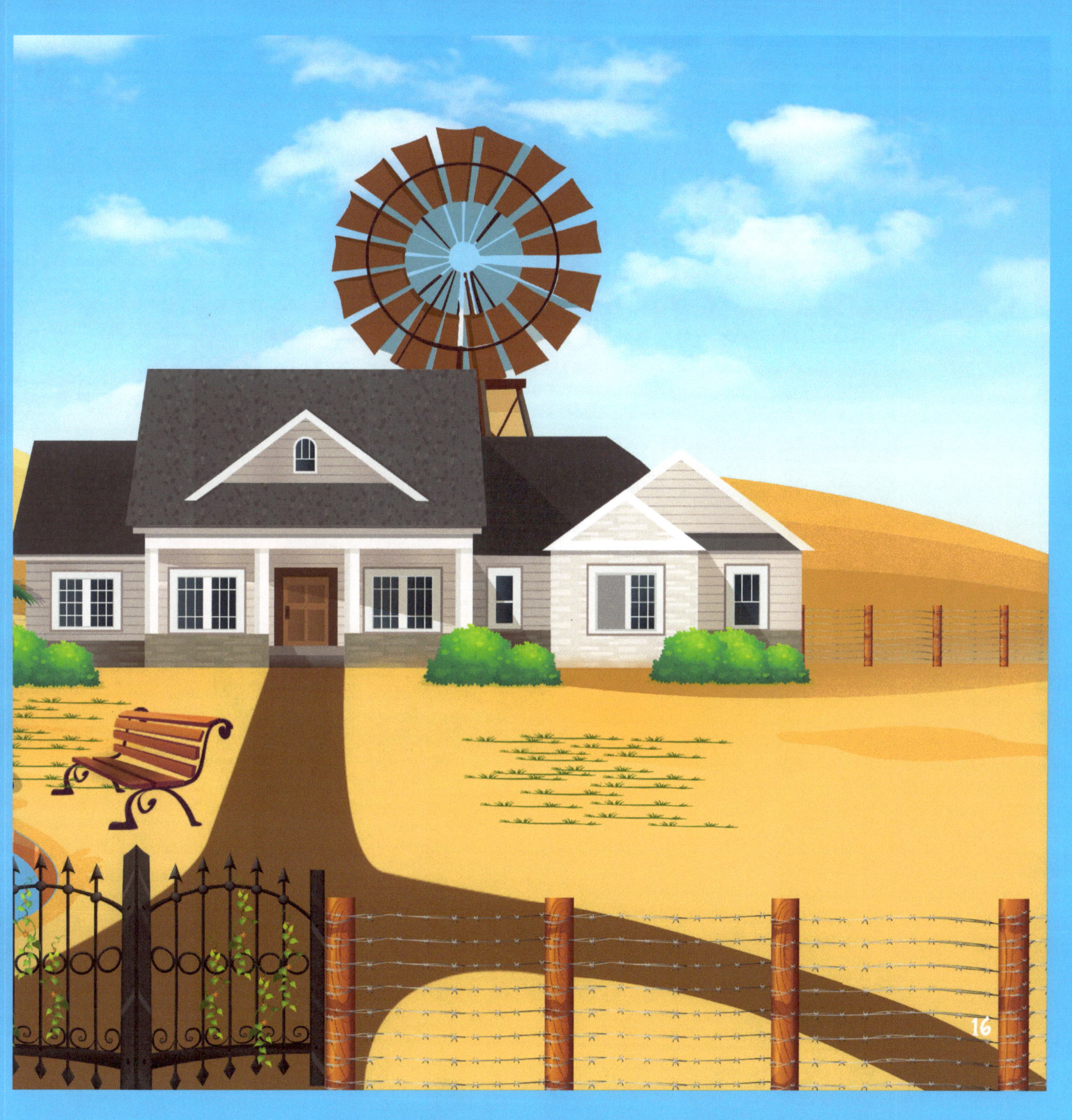

Mama must have flown over the fence and called to her babies to join her. They were so tiny that they could fit through the barbed-wire fence and get out. Not so for the 7th duckling.

The old lady was worried. The 7th duckling could not quack, and she could not fly. It was August. Fall and winter are coming.

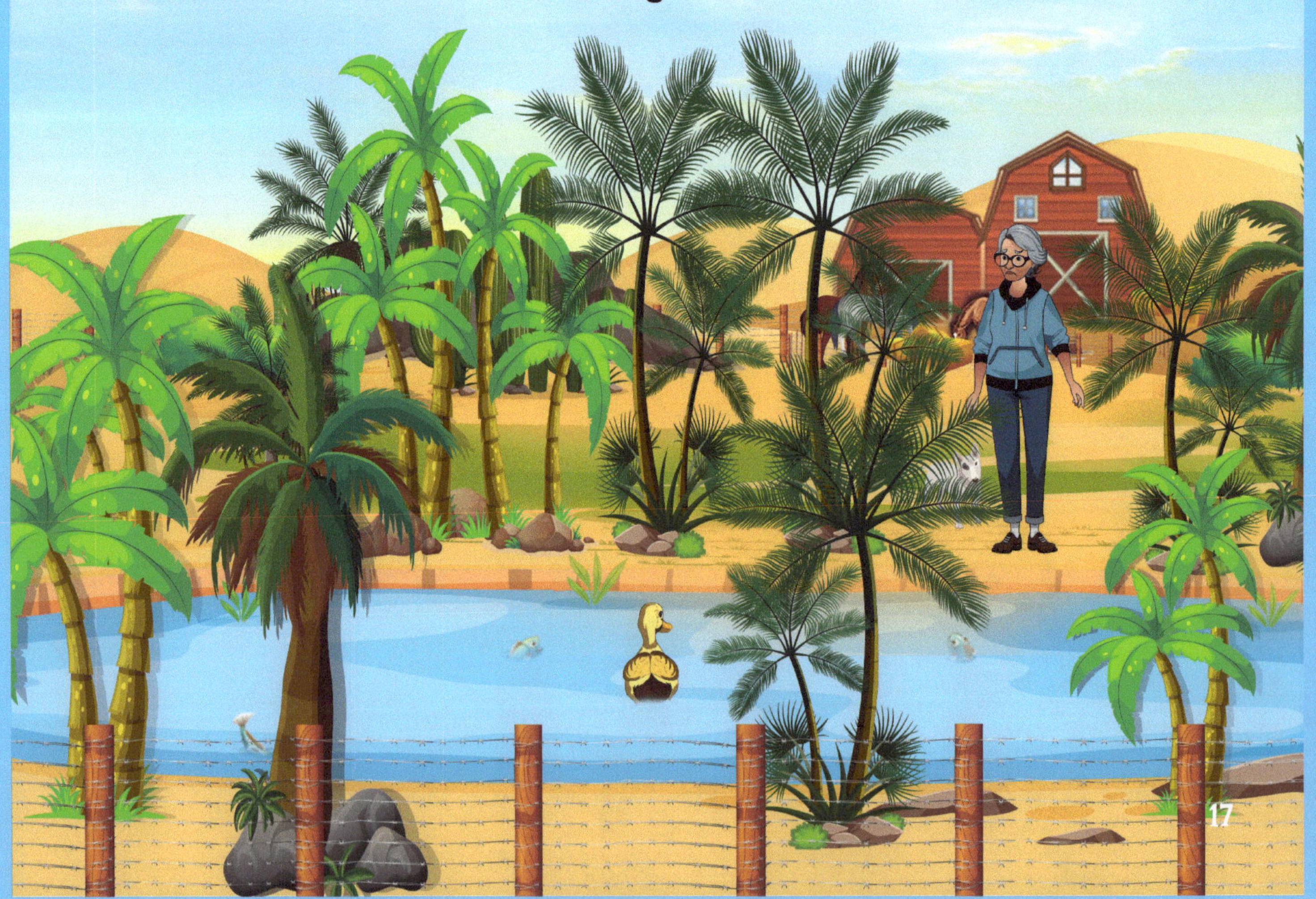

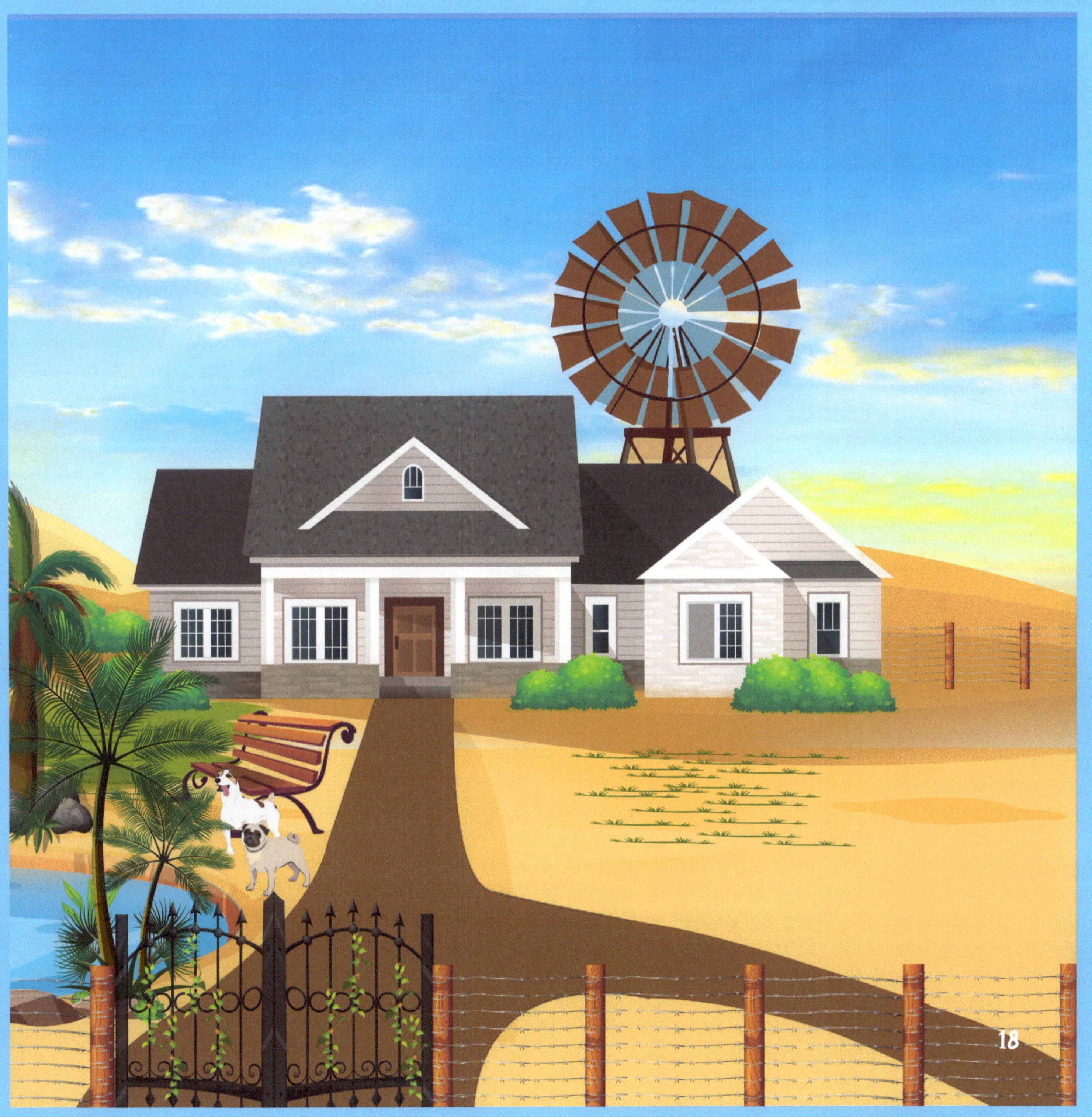

18

Each morning, the old lady would look for Mama and the other ducks, but they didn't come back. She sat on the bench near the pond. She wasn't worried about the 7th duckling getting food, but was it good enough? She went to the local grain store and found out you could feed chicken scratch to ducklings to make sure they got all their vitamins. She bought some, put it in a shallow pie pan, and placed it on the ground near the pond.

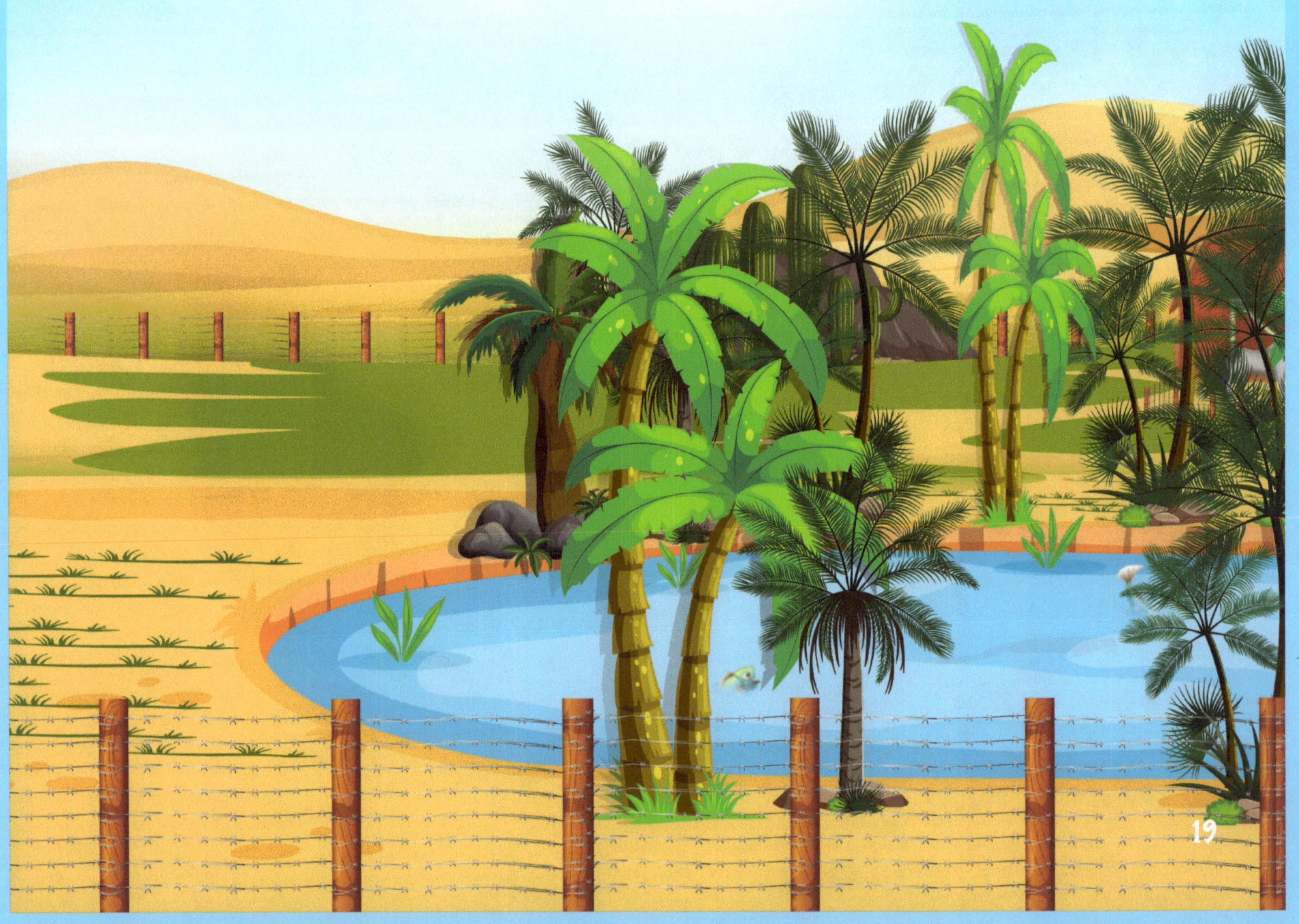

19

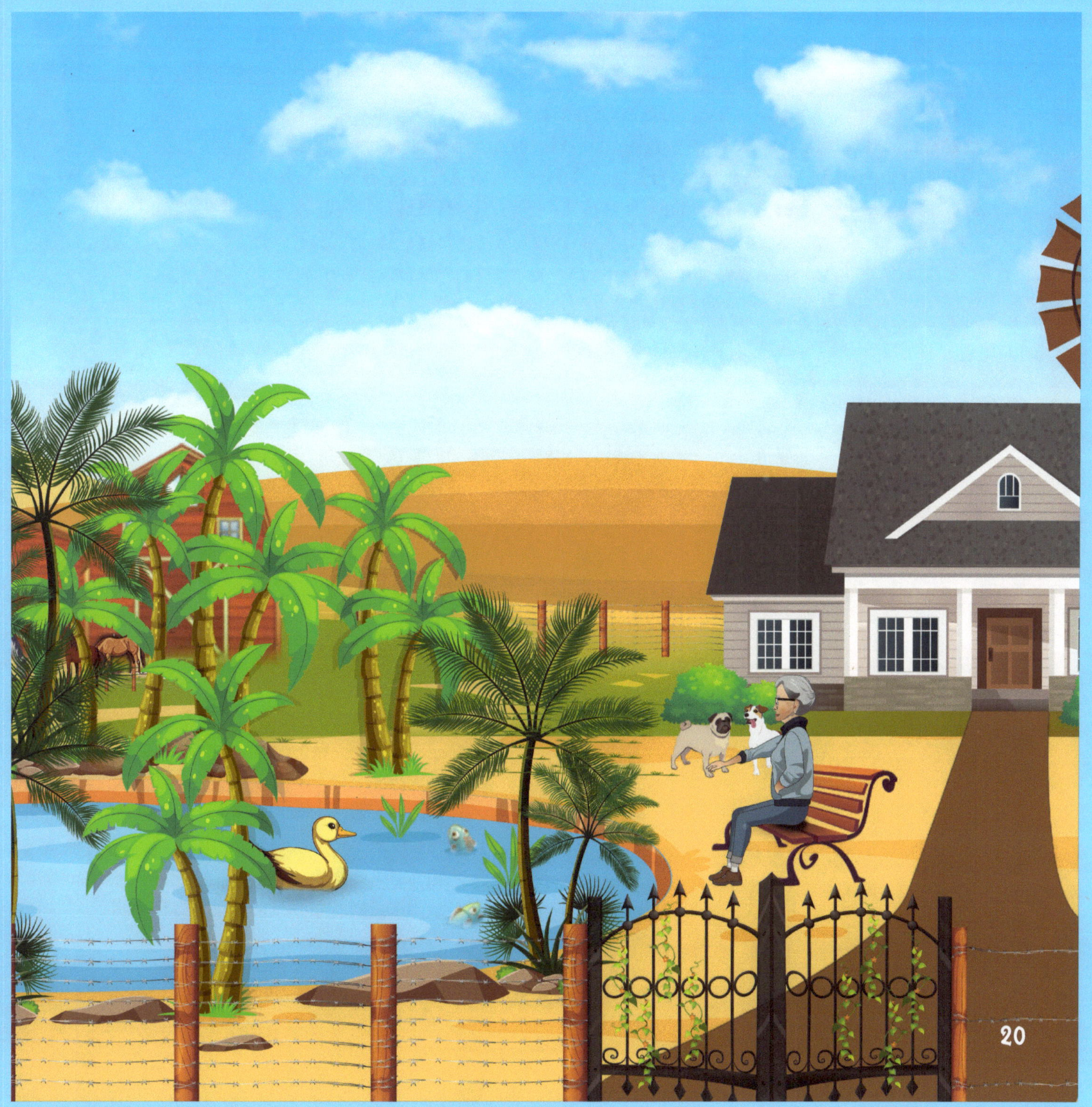

The next day, she was surprised to see the duckling near the pan, looking right at her, because it was empty. The old lady sat on the bench and wondered if she should name this duck, build a house for her, bring her into her own house, or call a wildlife person.

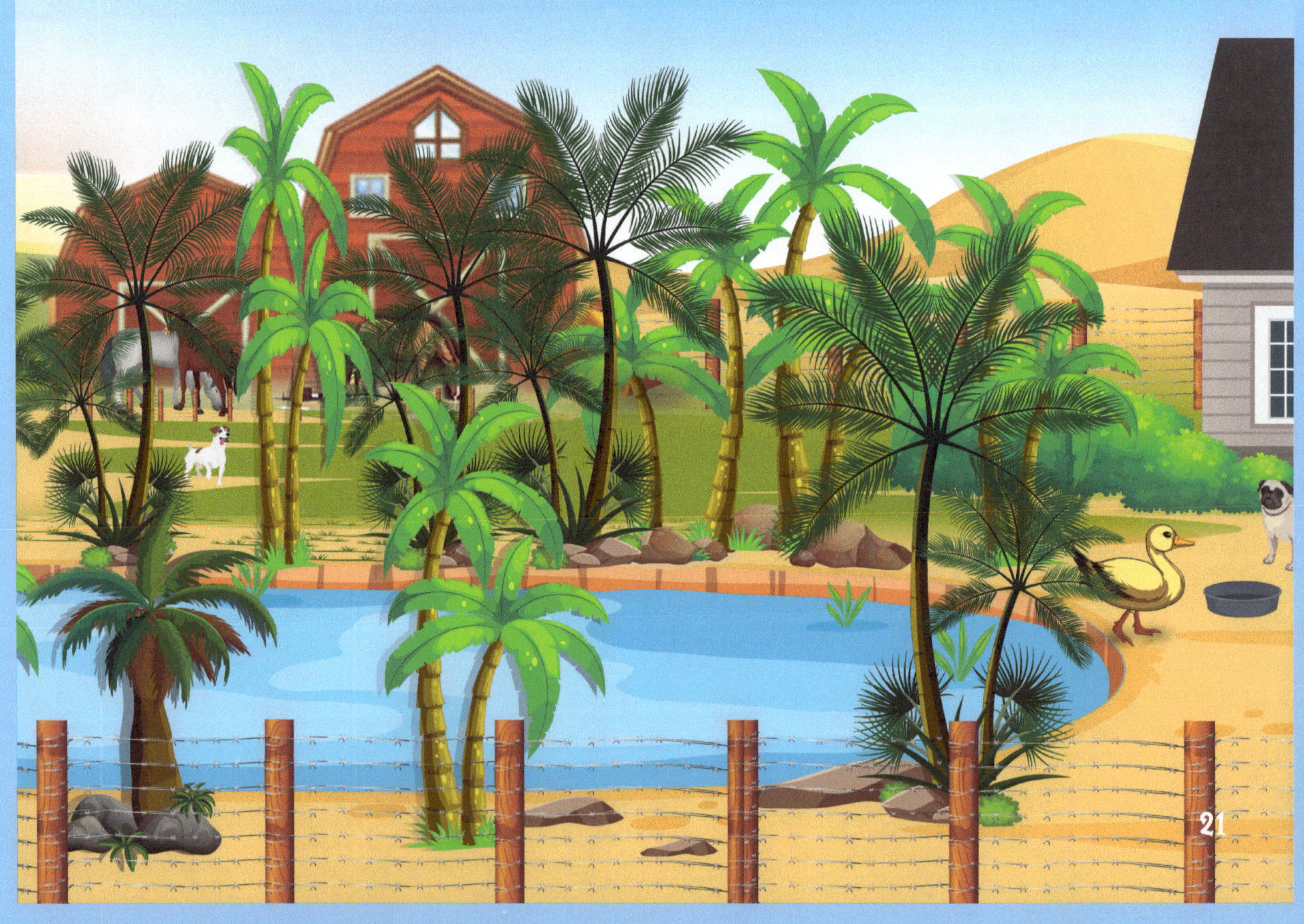

21

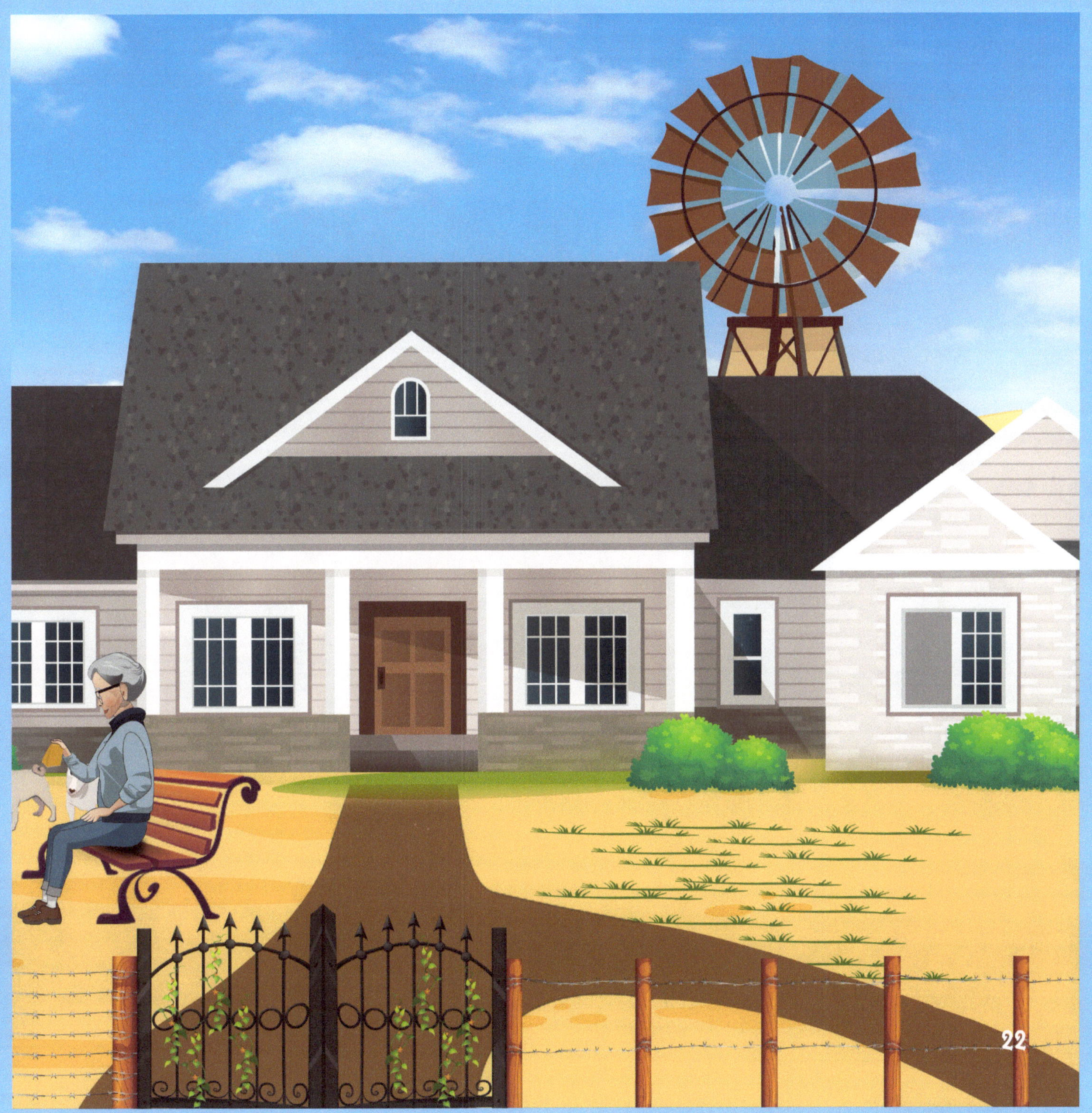

The old man and the old woman sat on the bench, wondering what to do with the duckling. She needs flying lessons, said the old lady. Oh, litttle ducklings, what will we do with you? The old man spoke up and said, Oh, little duckling; flying lessons are coming your way.

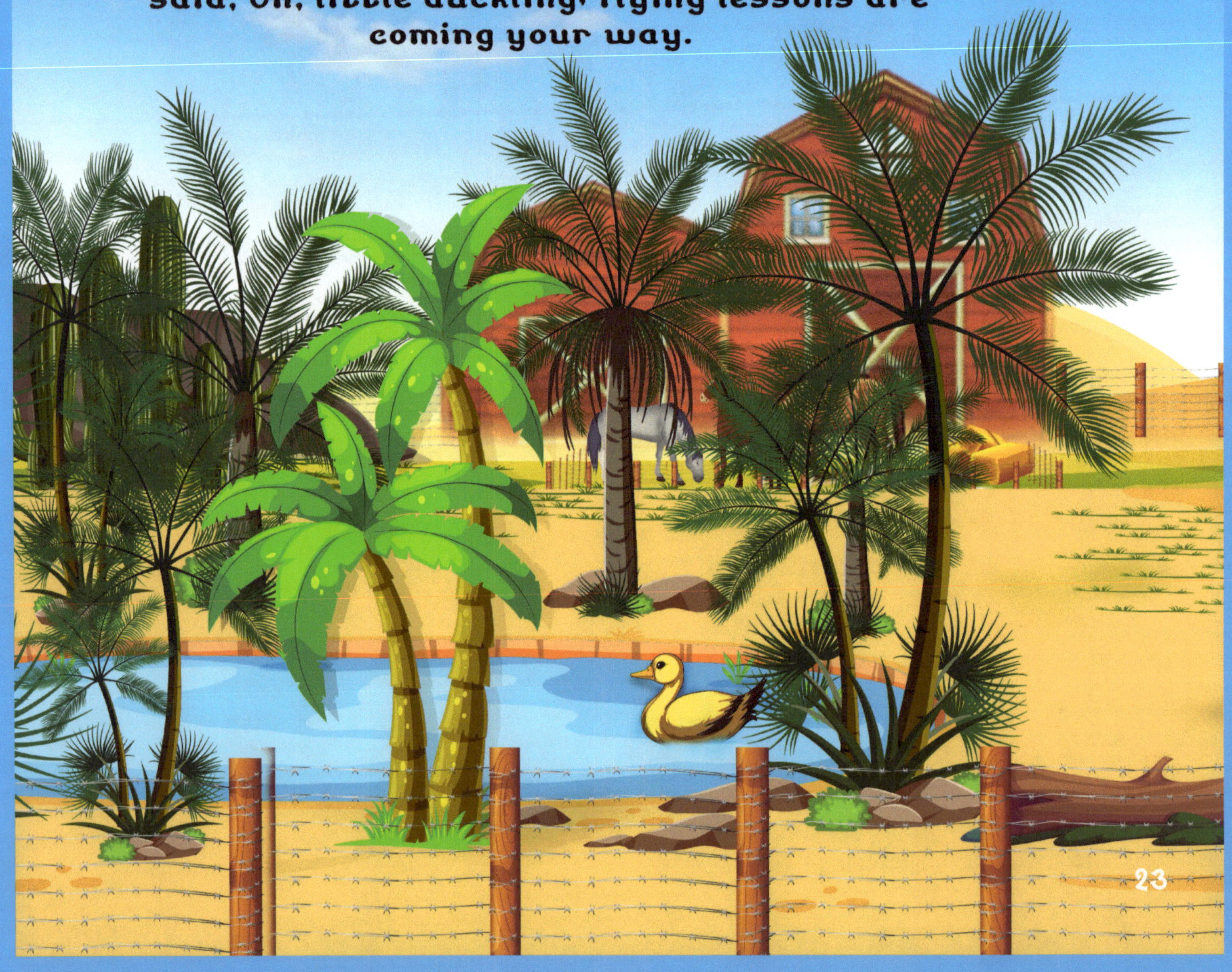

23

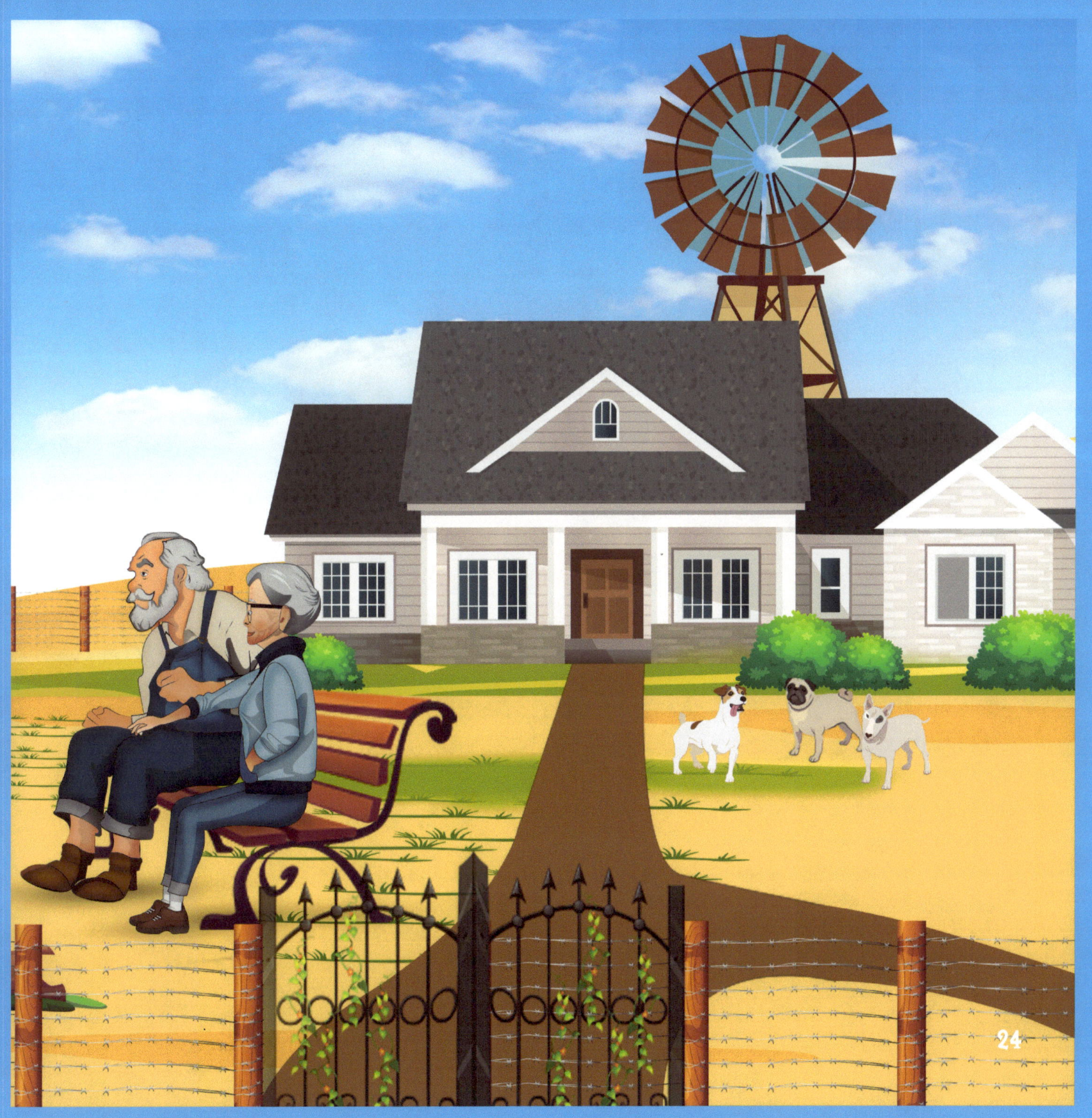

EXPLORE THE STORIES FURTHER AT
WRITERS-VILLAGE.COM, WHERE
HEARTWARMING BOOKS FOR CHILDREN
AND FAMILIES AWAIT.

www.ingramcontent.com/pod-product-compliance
Lightning Source LLC
Chambersburg PA
CBHW042135030726
47599CB00002B/484